HOW TO SURVIVE
HOSPITAL CARE

It all started with Norman Cousins and his blockbuster book, *Anatomy of An Illness*. Fighting a crippling disease in the hospital, Cousins would con his nurse into pulling the shades and projecting old Marx Brothers movies.

It was his contention that ten minutes of belly laughs had an anesthetic effect that would provide two hours of pain–free sleep.

Now, thanks to the new science of humor physiology know as Gelotology, researchers have concluded that humor plays a vital role in the recovery of most hospital patients.

Laughter raises your pulse rate and blood pressure, which aids circulation, strengthens the heart, and clears mucus from the lungs. It also does miracles for morale, the ague and the pip.

Says Dr. Ann Kiessling of the Harvard Medical Center, "People who get a hoot out of life spend less time in the hospital. Giving vent to some belly laughs will have a most salubrious effect, especially when the hospital bill is delivered."

Sooner or later most of us will face the foreboding portals of a hospital ward. The purpose of this humble effort is to guide you through them with a stuff upper lip and a song in your heart.

HOW TO SURVIVE
HOSPITAL CARE

or

"Why They Keep Bedpans In The Freezer"

WILLIAM C. ANDERSON

LEGENDARY PUBLISHING COMPANY
BOISE, IDAHO

Library of Congress Catalog Card Number: 95–080408

International Standard Book Number: 1–887747–00–1

First Printing: January, 1996

Illustrations by: Scott Anderson
Edited by: Jean Terra
Design & Layout: Richard Terra/Terra Nova

LEGENDARY PUBLISHING COMPANY
Lorry Roberts, Publisher
P.O. Box 7706
Boise, Idaho 83707–1706

Printed in the United States of America by:
Gilliland Printing, Inc., Arkansas City, Kansas

This book is available at special discounts for bulk purchases for sales promotions, premiums and for fund–raising. For details, contact Legendary Publishing by telephone at 800–358–1929.

ACKNOWLEDGMENTS

This author would be sorely remiss if certain contributors to this weighty tome were not properly acknowledged:

Mr. Norman Cousins, whose best–selling *Anatomy of An Illness* extols the virtues of laughter and an upbeat attitude as major contributors to the healing process, and which became the inspiration for this modest compendium.

Becky, Shari, Mary, Yvonne, Susan, and all the other white–smocked angels of mercy with whom I fell madly in love while frolicking through open heart surgery.

And above all, my red–headed lover, masseuse, TLC provider, chief cook, home–maker, laugher–at–my–dumb–jokes, and all–around beautiful human being – my wife, Dortha.

CONTENTS

FOREWORD

With the possible exception of a rectal root canal, or an Internal Revenue Service audit by a revenuer suffering from acute hemorrhoids, there is probably nothing more traumatic than finding oneself enrolled in one of our nation's infirmaries.

Whether preparing to deliver oneself of a baby, a tumor, part of one's anatomy, or in response to the symptoms of some unpronounceable disease, the news of an impending sojourn in the hospital ranks right up there with the pronouncement that one's brother–in–law is moving in for good.

By far the best method of checking into a medical

facility is through some type of physical misfortune that involves ambulances, emergency equipment, and high–speed chases through rush–hour traffic. In this way, one is so preoccupied with wailing sirens, squealing tires, and white–smocked strangers doing unspeakable things with one's torso, that even the antiseptic halls of an Emergency Ward look good.

For those less fortunate, however, who are compelled to check into a medical sanctorum through normal, non–emergency channels, there are a couple of ways to do it. Probably the best way is to bite the bullet, or maybe a Valium pill or two, and be marched into Admittance at gunpoint. This way is generally more acceptable than getting sloshed to the eyeballs to muster the courage to face the Admittance clerk. There have been instances when users of the latter method have ended up in the drunk tank, which can be almost as much fun as ending up in a hospital ward.

But regardless of the circumstances surrounding one's check–in to a medical facility, sooner or later almost everyone will have to enter the forbidding portals. The purpose of this modest compendium, therefore, is to help smooth the way for the uninitiated, to explain the often–times perplexing methods employed by hospitals and their staffs, and to provide comfort and solace to those donning a hospital gown. Hospitals can, indeed, be a heap of fun.

A careful study of this "How–To" handbook, and digestion of the many facts and recommendations expressed herein, will help prepare the reader for that hospital visit. Armed with this knowledge, one may not only be able to survive hospital care, but find it downright enjoyable. Not only is breakfast served in bed, there are always those fetching hospital gowns.

The trick is, always think of the bright side. It is the author's fervent hope that this conspectus will help the reader do just that.

The Emergency Ward is

a fun place to meet people.

HOW TO SURVIVE
HOSPITAL CARE

THE THRILL
OF GETTING ADMITTED

As stated in the Foreword, by far the best way to get admitted to a hospital is through the Emergency Ward. You still have to go through all the paperwork, but with any luck, you can do it lying down on a gurney.

Even this method is not foolproof, however, for in Emergency Wards of major metropolitan hospitals, it is not uncommon to have to wait in a line of gurneys extending clear to Cleveland. Which brings up a very important point: electing to have a medical emergency in a large metropolitan area shows poor planning. The Emergency Wards in large cities have all the ambiance of a bus depot, with just about the same attention to the client's care and comfort.

There are few things more discomfiting than checking into a trauma center with a chicken bone in your throat only to find you've stumbled into the aftermath of a gang war being waged by the Bloods and the Entrails. In which case you may emerge from the hospital with more medical problems than you had going in.

So, properly planning one's emergencies to transpire in localities less densely populated is the first step toward more pacific medical attention. Or, if you don't have a genuine emergency, you might fake one. Like Judea Ipswitch of Perth Amboy, New Jersey. As a result of a football injury, Judea was blessed with a very life–like artificial leg. Judea was not above smearing it with catsup, throwing it over his shoulder, and crutching into Emergency. This did not fool the hospital staff for long, but it did generally get him to the head of the flu–shot line.

Do not do like Armbruster Hammerhead of the

Bronx, who flung himself prostrate in front of the Intensive Care Unit of a New York hospital. People stepped over him for five days before someone finally noticed the arrow sticking out of his back, and lugged him into the Trauma Center.

It is not necessarily the end of the world, however, if you have to go through ambulatory channels to get admitted. Although it *was* the end of the world for Amelia Przybsz of Detroit, Michigan, who checked in with Poison Ivy rash. She unhappily expired on page six of the medical questionnaire while listing Childhood Diseases.

And it has been said, although never really verified, that Ms. Bambina Broccoli of Philadelphia set some kind of record in filling out admissions forms. She came into the hospital admissions office very pregnant, had a bouncing baby boy in the hospital lobby, and it had its first tooth before Bambina's paperwork was finally completed and she was assigned a bed in the maternity ward.

Seldom mentioned is the case of John Senior, Jr.,

a television personality in Brooklyn, who couldn't get admitted to the hospital because he was sick. It seemed that John Senior, Jr., had a contagious disease called "Hoof and Mouth," a malady often contracted by talk–show hosts. The hapless man was quarantined to the taxi cab that had delivered him to the Mother of Mercy Hospital, and he spent three weeks riding through the streets of Brooklyn before he was well enough to be admitted.

Before you have earned the neatly–lettered plastic bracelet affixed to your wrist, however, there is more to be done than just surmounting the mountain of paperwork. You must show documented proof that you are able to pay for the medical attention you are about to receive. And I mean *pay!* It may also come as a shock that many hospitals no longer accept wampum or brightly colored beads; doctor's bills can no longer be satisfied with a couple of chickens, a nice fat pig, or a dozen jars of homemade succotash.

So if you do not possess medical insurance, are

not a member of OPEC, or are not a paramour of Donald Trump, you will have a better chance of winning the Bangladesh lottery than being admitted to one of our havens for the medically distressed.

And above all, do not be intimidated by the thick rugs in the hospital lobby, the expensive artwork on its walls, or the fact that the parking lot reserved for doctors is filled with Alfa Romeos and Rolls Royces. For some reason the cost of medical care seems to just keep rising.

But you have now survived the blizzard of paperwork, have been assigned a hospital bed, and with eager anticipation you head for your ward.

What bliss awaits!

Accessories make the hospital gown even more fetching.

FETCHING WAYS TO WEAR
YOUR HOSPITAL GOWN

lthough checking into hospitals via the emergency route while bleeding profusely is generally accepted as the most desirable, it is not without its drawbacks.

When you go wheeling in through the emergency doors of a hospital, it matters not your ailment. Be it a fishhook in the scalp, a sprained toe, or a problem caused by inadvertently serving mai tais made with Raid instead of rum, the standing medical procedure is the same: all of your clothes must be removed.

And this does not mean simply disrobing. Good hospital practice demands that clothing must always be cut off with a pair of very long shears. Basil

Crapster of Yonkers, New York, checked into a hospital trauma center with an aching hangnail. "I had on my new executive slacks, a $100 silk shirt, and an Italian necktie. The pants had a well–functioning zipper, the shirt had buttons, and the shoes had laces. It took longer to scissor my clothes off than it would have taken to unzip and unbutton. Okay, I can understand the panic of the moment. But did they also have to cut the laces in my shoes and clip my fifty–buck tie? I'm convinced the medics are in cahoots with the garment industry."

From this comes another very worthwhile tip: whenever possible, have your emergencies while wearing old clothes. Adds Hugh Pugh of Bangor, Maine, a veteran of hospital emergencies, "I thought I had it made when I checked in with a bad case of heartburn. I had just come from a masquerade party and was wearing a suit of armor. Aha! I thought to myself, just watch those suckers try to scissor this outfit." He sighed. "You ever been opened up with an acetylene torch?"

Another unfortunate victim, Joe Passwater, a telephone repairman from Sandusky, Ohio, reports, "You've got to be damned careful going through the doors of any emergency room. It happened in Sandusky when I was attacked by those damn white–smocked scissorbills. Before I knew what had happened, my pants had been ripped off, my shirt was in shreds, and I damned near had my second circumcision. That ain't no way to treat a guy who just went in to fix the phone!"

And finally, rounding out this documentation is the testimony of Melody Bang, an actress from Burbank, California, who was testifying at a malpractice suit against a doctor who had performed a bust enhancement operation on her. He had allegedly closed up the incisions, leaving not only three sponges, but his wedding ring and the car keys to his Mercedes Benz in her left breast. This was discovered when Melody tried to go through airport security and blew out all the landing lights in the Burbank airport. Testifies Miss Bang, "Maybe they had to cut off my jumpsuit on the operating table, but my new bra? My boyfriend can remove it with absolutely no trouble standing on his head in a sunken canoe."

It is not until you are shorn of your raiments, however, that the fun part begins. As if to atone for the high-handed measures employed by the wielders of the sheep shears, the hospital staff makes a presentation guaranteed to impress the most jaded hospital enrollee. This, of course, being the hospital gown.

Like so many mysteries whirling around the medical profession, the reason for the adoption of the hospital gown has never been explained—least of all by the medical staff. This backless robe was obviously designed by a committee including the Marquis de Sade and Gypsy Rose Lee. It fits like a straight-jacket, being tied in back with a cord around the neck that is credited with throttling more people than the Hillside Strangler.

Something has to be worn under this ode to medical splendor, unless you are exceptionally proud of your derriere, for it hangs out as naked as a plucked dodo bird for all the world to see. The gown comes in many sizes, except the size you wear, which always happens to be in the laundry. Were it not for its fetching color—dishwater gray—the universal hospital gown would have very little to recommend it.

The drawbacks to the typical hospital garb have been described by Augustus J. Feeblebunny, who relates this incident at the Cedars Sinai Hospital in Los Angeles. "I was relaxing on a gurney waiting my turn to go into the room used for cardiac catheterization. Suddenly, out of the door bolted a portly man wearing nothing but his hospital gown, which was flowing behind him like the veils of Salome. From the rear, he presented the picture of a naked, well–endowed posterior that could have been created only by a dedicated couch potato.

"Out of the swinging doors in hot pursuit came two medics, armed with hypodermic needles. The trio sped down the corridor, turned a corner, and disappeared. When it came time for me to enter the cardiac catheterization chamber, I queried my attendant as to the reason for the high–speed chase down the halls. I was told that the gentleman had decided he didn't want to have a long tube stuck up his groin, threaded up a vein and into his heart where it would release a spurt of dye that could be photographed by X–ray cameras. When I entered that chamber I was sorely tempted to join him for the room resembled nothing more than Doctor Frankenstein's laboratory.

"It turned out that the patient eluded pursuit, only to end up in the Beverly Hills police station, where he was booked for indecent exposure. It is probably high time that medics design a new hospital gown if they are going to continue developing new equipment that scares the hell out of patients. A gown, at least, that if worn in public will not guarantee a trip to the slammer."

As all well–dressed people know, no wardrobe is complete without a little adornment. Since your valu-

WHY HOSPITAL WARDS
ARE SO DARN MUCH FUN

This section will prove invaluable in helping you to come to grips with normal hospital routine. Before expanding on this subject, however, it should be noted that two prerequisites should be developed by the patient at this point:

1. A great sense of humor. Otherwise, you may not fully appreciate the many fun things that go on in your hospital ward.

2. A good attitude.

By developing a positive attitude, you can look at the bright side of hospital care. You get to have breakfast in bed, you do not have to cook, do the dishes, do housework, or even make your own bed.

It should be remembered that staying one day in even the cheapest hospital costs about three times as much as spending a day on a first–class cruise ship, so you should certainly get the maximum enjoyment out of your hospital stay.

To help the present–day patient know what to expect, we will now go hand–in–hand through a normal day of hospital routine.

2:15 AM. You should have just gotten to sleep when the night nurse comes in, shines her flashlight in your face, and shakes you until you are wide awake. She then asks if you have taken your sleeping pill.

3:30 AM. You have just slipped back into merciful repose when the patient in the next bed rolls over in his sleep and lands on the TV control button. The television set comes on at eight zillion decibels while James Arness shoots the hell out of Tombstone.

4:52 AM. There is a hellacious clatter on the roof as the emergency helicopter lands on the chopper pad. Feverish activity ensues, as a man who has just tried to swallow his Harley Davidson motorcycle is wheeled into your ward.

6:00 AM. Just about the time you have finally dropped off to sleep again, you are awakened by your nurse bearing a water basin full of cold water and a washcloth, with instructions to wash up before breakfast. What she doesn't tell you is that breakfast will arrive promptly three hours later.

6:15 AM. A physical therapist appears with a Rube Goldberg contraption into which you have to inhale and exhale vigorously. This ostensibly is to prevent pneumonia but is used even on patients who come in for a tummy tuck. Physical therapists make more money than Oprah Winfrey.

6:30 AM. You have just nodded back to sleep when a yawning orderly comes in to take a sample of your blood. Hospitals have devised an insidious secret alarm that alerts a member of the blood bank who comes running on the double whenever a patient nods off to sleep. It's a little known fact that most hospitals defray spiraling medical expenses by selling bat guano to kumquat growers. Which explains why you'll find bat caves in the basements of most hospitals. Unfortunately, bats are voracious little critters and must be fed half–a–dozen times a day. And since bats like human blood, you know why veins must be poked on an hourly basis.

6:47 AM. The ninety–year–old man in the next room is talking in his sleep. It seems he was admitted with a buckshot implant delivered by a jealous husband and he chuckles a lot as he relives the events leading up to his injury.

7:22 AM. You have just dropped off to sleep again when the nurse comes to measure the peepee in your plastic urinal and ask embarrassing questions about your bowel movements. You will always be advised to drink more liquids, even if you have just expelled enough to float the QE–2. And the less said about BMs the better.

7:35 AM. You are nodding off again when the nurse comes in with your pills. Ranging the spectrum from pea–size to golf–ball–size, pills like to roll around a lot, and much time is spent on the floor tracking down the elusive medication that has missed your mouth. In such an advanced and sophisticated profession as medicine, it has never been fully explained why the medics have yet to come up with the square pill.

8:20 AM. Once again you are just cozying up in the arms of Morpheus when your doctor comes in. He gives you a $42 handshake, claps you on the back, tells you you should get more sleep, and departs before you've had a chance to tell him he has called you by the wrong name.

9:00 AM. You have given up trying to sleep and have just tackled a crossword puzzle. Your breakfast arrives. The fact that it was mixed up with the meal for the no–salt, no–fat, no–sugar patient in the next ward is not mentioned, for by this time you're so hungry you eat the napkin, the doily, and the next day's menu.

9:02 AM. The arrival of your tray is the signal for

the simultaneous arrival of the blood–taker, the therapist with the Rube Goldberg inhaler, the patient from the next ward demanding to know why you are eating his breakfast, and the nurse who proceeds to strip your bed.

10:17 AM. You have just curled up for a quick nap when the nurse announces it's bath time. As she closes the curtains around your bed, she hands you a washbasin with the same instructions delivered by Florence Nightingale, "I'll wash down as far as possible, up as far as possible, and you wash possible." This is always accompanied by much thigh–slapping hilarity as the nurse splashes soapsuds all over your clean sheets.

12:00 Noon. Time for lunch. Lunch doesn't come, but a volunteer candy–striper pushing a reading cart does. On the cart are a dozen Nancy Drew books, several magazines with no covers, and a bunch of novels written by someone named Barbara Cartland. There is nothing readable, but the candy–striper giggles and blushes a lot and is so cute you overlook the bubble gum in her hair.

1:45 PM. Lunch comes. You wish it hadn't.

3:02 PM. Feeding time for the bats, so the white–smocked vampire swoops down bearing a big grin and a blunt needle.

3:30 PM. You have just entered dreamland only to find your repose is shattered by all manner of people trooping in for Visiting Hour. This is when you discover that your roommate in the next bed is a scoutmaster. A large part of Boy Scout Troop 57 is now roosting on your bed while an Eagle Scout demonstrates the art of improvised campfire–starting by setting fire to your wastepaper basket.

4:42 PM. Your spouse appears, bringing you the bills from the daily mail. You are informed that everything is going along fine in your absence. Fortunately, the house was insured and very little damage was done by the firemen who came in to put out the blaze started by the curtains that ignited from the candles on the bier of your dog who was unfortunately in the garage when your spouse drove through the garage door in a hurry to get to the IRS auditors who had just slapped a lien on the house and were putting up a For Sale sign.

5:55 PM. Your spouse leaves, suffering from a spell of nausea. Even though you warned her not to, she had removed the warming cover from your dinner that had just arrived.

7:18 PM. The members of Boy Scout Troop 57 have folded their tents and departed, along with your basket of fruit that had been sent by a buddy as a last–ditch effort to help you ward off starvation.

9:02 PM. Visiting hours are now over, and the babble of visitors has been replaced by the ca-cophony of the ward's 82 television sets all being tuned to different channels.

10:02 PM. The bat–feeder arrives, and while drawing blood wants to know why you have a pillow over your head.

11:05 PM. The day nurse comes in to tuck you in and say goodnight, as she is turning you over to the night nurse. She admonishes you to get more rest, and gives you a sleeping pill.

2:15 AM. You have just gotten to sleep when the night nurse comes in, shines her flashlight in your face, and shakes you until you're wide awake. She then asks if you are sleeping all right.

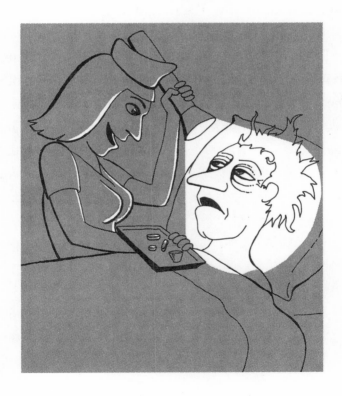

This 24–hour calendar, with minor variations, is typical of the fun–filled days you may look forward to during your hospital stay. As previously stated, hospital tours may not be enjoyed to the maximum unless one maintains a good attitude and a rollicking sense of humor. Keeping this in mind will certainly add to the pleasure of a hospital vacation.

Just remember, it's costing you at least three times as much a day as an ocean cruise. Approached with the right attitude, it can certainly be as much fun.

And with any luck at all, you may not even get seasick.

NEVER SHAKE HANDS
WITH A PROCTOLOGIST

The following pronouncement will come as no surprise to veteran medical patients: Most doctors are functionally illiterate.

In this day and age, there are few job opportunities for people who can neither read nor write. Which is a shame, as this limitation has caused a rather scurrilous segment of our society to enter the medical profession, where literacy is not a prerequisite.

Doctors try to mask this deficiency in any number of ways, but anyone who has ever tried to decipher a medical prescription will agree that the hen–scratchings are completely illegible to everyone, including pharmacists.

And, as everyone knows, doctors and pharmacists have long been in cahoots. So it doesn't matter what kind of hieroglyphics doctors put on their prescriptions, druggists can't read them anyway. Actually, prescriptions are ordered over the telephone by the doctor's nurse using a very complicated code. Since it takes a good deal of time for a nurse to learn this code, not to mention the time the druggist must spend deciphering it, this explains why a box of aspirin cost about the same as a Stealth B–2 Bomber.

But the intellectual inadequacies of one's doctor should not color a patient's attitude. Most medical men are wealthy, gregarious, socially acceptable and lots of fun. In getting to know your physician, you should be aware of the following traits that are prevalent among people wearing a stethoscope (and do not be fooled by this badge of the medical profession. It is used primarily to open beer bottles and to root around in the cleavage of well–endowed females).

All doctors wear Gucci shoes, Italian suits and

drive a Mercedes Benz. They are very personable and charming because they know this is the best way to butter up a patient they are about to slap with a bill that would underwrite foreign aid for the developing nations. It is advisable never to shake hands with a doctor, especially proctologists.

Doctors are very busy. They not only have to meet with their brokers, schedule golf games, attend seminars in either Hawaii or Las Vegas (for some reason seminars are never held in Molting Moose, Alaska), give physicals to new nurses, and if there is any time left over, make hospital rounds and schedule patients. As for the latter, all doctors take their cues from the airlines and overbook their appointments. Their rationale is that at least one or two of their patients will drop dead before their appointment, which will help absorb the overflow.

An illustration of how busy medics really are comes to us from Felicia Funbuns of Walla Walla, Washington, who was in the hospital for a nipple transplant. "I was somewhat surprised," says Ms.

Funbuns, "when this family of five moved into the ward in the beds next to mine. I thought they might have contracted some kind of contagious disease but everyone appeared so healthy. And then I discovered the reason. It seems the family's father was a pediatrician and was so busy he never got home. So the family just checked into the ward, bag and baggage, and now they get to see the father at least once a day when he makes his hospital rounds. According to the doctor's wife, this has worked out fine as the good doctor now even calls his children by their right names."

However, not all medics are quite so family–oriented. In fact, more so than in any other profession with the possible exception of aluminum–siding salesmen, doctors have quite a reputation for being "Womanizers." Male doctors, that is. Female doctors are known as "Menninites," which explains why they have buttons on their pantyhose and like to zip around town in horse–drawn carriages.

Surgeons, being a member in more or less good

standing of the medical fraternity, are also functionally illiterate but they seem to be a bit handier than
physicians. After taking workshop in trade school,
the students who proved handiest with electrical
saws, drills, and ball–peen hammers go on to become surgeons. You can always spot surgeons because they generally have one or two fingers missing and they all drive Porsches.

All doctors, regardless of their specialty, like to
talk in the third person. Especially when you're lying prone on a gurney or hospital bed, you suddenly
become an inanimate object. Guenivere Gargle of
Placenta, Pennsylvania sums it up neatly. "My rela-
tions with Doctor Scrubb were great until I was op-
erated on, then I suddenly became a side of beef.
Doc would make his rounds with a couple of interns
and instead of saying 'Hi, Gwen,' he referred to me
as a twenty–eight year old female Caucasian with a
history of tropical fungus whose ventrical bicustard
had become inflamed and the cuspidor had had to
be removed by an invasive probe through the ob-

longata. Then, to add insult to injury, he'd throw up my gown and show everybody my scar, including the florist who'd just delivered a chrysanthemum plant."

Adds Horace Hotloins of Murky Water, Massachusetts, "Just because you're lying there on a stretcher, medics think you must be out of it. While lying on a gurney awaiting an angiogram in the Hallelujah Hospital of Murky Water, I heard two medics talking about their sex life, where the best Mercedes mechanics hang out, and how they wouldn't let the doctor who was tending me operate on their dog. When I tried to enter their conversation, they looked at me as if I were a training–aid cadaver. Medics are a queer breed."

One last facet of the medical profession that should be touched upon to help with your understanding of these gowned masochists who like to attack your torso with all manner of hideous instruments: Doctors are not to be taken too seriously when they plead poverty and pontificate about the terrible financial hardships imposed upon them by Medicare, Medicaid, and other insurance carriers who want to pay them far less for their laying on of medical hands than the doctors think they deserve.

Says Clara Clapsaddle, recovering from a bosom implant in an Oshkosh, Wisconsin hospital, "Maybe it was a silly operation, having a large breast implanted in the middle of my back, but it was my boyfriend's birthday and he likes to dance a lot. Anyway, I was surprised to find that my insurance didn't cover the operation and so was my plastic surgeon. I felt so sorry for him, we organized a little charity benefit. We had it on his yacht anchored at his winter place in Cannes. Happily, we cleared enough to cover his expenses."

On the off–chance you will ever get to engage in conversation with your doctor for longer than thirty seconds, you will find the term "malpractice insurance" surfaces about every third sentence. It is true that in today's litigious society, doctors are being sued by irate patients at the drop of a stitch. Ergo, insurance premiums to cover malpractice suits are at an all–time high.

Case in point: Says Hamhock McGoon of Chicken, Alaska, "I never ever even thought of suing anyone. But when I went into the Dawson City Hospital with a kidney stone and came out with a hysterectomy, it was a little much. Not too many men in Alaska have hysterectomies, and since I'm a professional wrestler it shot my image all to hell. I hated to sue ole Doc Haggerty just because his bifocals fell into the instrument sterilizer and he couldn't see, but he shoulda stopped the operation. I had to get some kinda compensation 'cause who in hell's gonna wrestle with a guy who's had a hysterectomy?"

"It's a shame the cost of medical insurance is so high," says Daphne Dimbulb of Swill, Illinois, "and I know doctors are under great pressure. But even so, they've got to be more careful. I know things are hectic here in our huge metropolitan hospitals, but there's no excuse for checking in with a tummy tumor and checking out with a twelve–pound baby.

"Never hire a plastic surgeon with a drinking problem."

And do you know what they did to the woman across the hall? She went in with an infected sinus and came out with a tonsil implant. Doctors just have to lay off sniffing that happy gas."

Eustice P. Boondoggle, an insurance executive from Hen, Rhode Island, puts it this way. "I've settled a lot of weird malpractice claims, but one of the weirdest was that of the proctologist who was performing a colon operation and somehow managed to sew his patient's thumb to his rectum. Due to the criticality of the operation the doctor couldn't go back in and for ten days the patient ran around with his thumb up his—but I'm sure you don't want to hear the grisly details."

And thus we have an insight into the chief medical practitioner who will help guide you through the medical ordeal you are facing. Just remember, medics are almost human (a few like to think more so) and most like to be treated as such. So by all means treat them kindly and courteously, don't make fun of any physical or mental aberrations they might possess, and always keep handy the name of a good attorney.

Following are some excellent words to live by concerning your doctor, and they should be committed to memory:

1. Never let an anesthesiologist who moonlights as a casket salesman near you.

2. Just prior to surgery, never call your doctor "Sawbones," "Witch Doctor" or "Medicine Man," and never, but never, mention his leech.

3. Never mention the fact that your doctor and the head nurse seem to spend a lot of time in the hospital morgue, even though it hasn't seen a body for weeks.

4. It is considered very tacky to ask your doctor if he wants his bill paid to his secret Swiss bank account.

5. It is considered good policy not to allude to your doctor's veterinarian training. Some doctors are sorely lacking in the humor department.

6. Be leery of a doctor who explains your upcoming operation by charting it out on a beef diagram used by butchers.

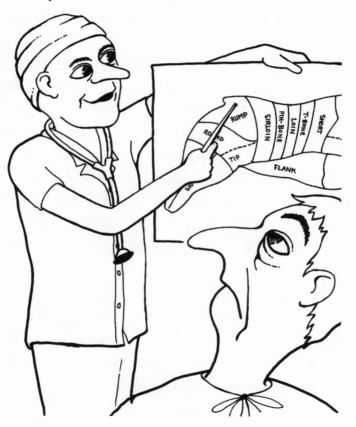

Close obeisance to these tips will serve you in good stead and do much to promote an amicable doctor/patient relationship.

After all, a person is about to attack your body with an array of very sharp instruments, generally when you are unconscious. It doesn't take a Rhodes Scholar to realize this is the last person in the world you want to pressure–load to an antagonistic position.

"Here's looking at you, kid."

WHEN NOT TO GROPE
YOUR NURSE

Female nurses come in all sizes, shapes, colors and dispositions. Most are compassionate, patient, skilled and worthy descendants of Florence Nightingale. A very few are diabolical, cantankerous, mean–spirited, do not trim their mustaches, and are direct descendants of Attila the Hun. There are also male nurses, but since they are definitely in the minority, we will touch upon them only in passing.

While doctors like to use the third person a lot, nurses speak only in the first person plural. It is always "How do *we* feel today?" Or, "Did *we* have a good BM this morning?" Or *"We* won't pour our grapefruit juice into our specimen jar again, will we?"

Nurses are generally much smarter than doctors, which is attested to by the fact that nurses can make a bed with a person in it—no small feat. Nurses are also generally prettier—although not always. Furthermore, patients bond with nurses more quickly and firmly than they do with doctors, for reasons already stated. It is difficult to strike up a warm and loving relationship with a doctor you see only once a day, and then just long enough for him to rip off your bandages.

Indeed, lots of people fall in love with their nurses. Says Cecil Slugbait of Chattahoochee, Florida, "My nurse had a face like a spoiled pomegranate and a personality like an open grave. But I dearly did love that woman. Maybe it's because I kept thinking hers would be the last face I'd ever see that it became very special. Or maybe it's the way she shaved me, or scrubbed my back in that first shower after my operation. Whatever it is, my wife doesn't understand why I still send my nurse flowers thirty–five years after my vasectomy."

Says Henrietta Hemstitch of Billings, Montana, "I had a male nurse. He had cold hands, the bedside manner of an aardvark, and breath that would stagger an ox. But I fell deeply in love with that man. Maybe it was the tender way he held my hand while shaving my head, but I'll always have a soft spot in my heart for my male nurse."

Nurses, like doctors, are human for the most part, and respond to thoughtfulness and consideration just like anyone else. So to this end, the following pointers, if heeded, will go far toward achieving the best possible patient/nurse relationship:

1. Regardless of the indignities heaped upon you by your nurse—and there will be many—keep a positive attitude. Always try to look at things from your nurse's point of view. She probably doesn't want to get involved in a Fleet's enema any more than you do.

2. This is where the novice patient often gets into

trouble and memorizing this one point will more than make the reading of this modest tome worthwhile: it is considered very gross to pass gas while your nurse is changing your sheets.

3. Asking friends to smuggle in alcoholic beverages in vases containing cut flowers is an old dodge, one that nurses are very familiar with. Likewise, nurses are trained to spot spirited contraband coming in disguised as Slushies, perfume, mouthwash and watermelons. A word to the wise will save a paragraph of embarrassment.

4. It is not good policy to practice your comedy routines while your private parts are being shaved. Some nurses have an uncontrollable sense of humor.

5. Groping your nurse while feigning medicational delusions is definitely a no–no.

6. If groping is called for, it should be done when the nurse is giving you a shower. Most anything can be blamed on slippery soap.

7. If your hospital is Catholic and your nurse is a nun, do not make bad jokes about getting her out of

44

NEVER EAT HOSPITAL
FOOD THAT CRAWLS

t is common knowledge that during World War Two, the last war we won, army cooks honed the production of unpalatable food to a fine art. What is not common knowledge is that they used a secret device called a De–appetizing Machine, specifically designed to turn good meat and vegetables into an indefinable glob that had only one claim to fame–it could fit into the compartments of a GI cafeteria tray.

Following the war, these war surplus machines were all snapped up by hospitals, where they once again perform the demanding job of turning fresh meat and vegetables into an unidentifiable glob that has only one claim to fame—it will fit into a hospital tray.

Adapting to the selling techniques of Madison Avenue, most hospitals now provide beautifully illustrated menus from which you can select your meals for the following day. Any similarity between the meal you actually receive and the picture of same depicted in the full-color menu is not only coincidental, it means you have received a tray intended for a member of the hospital staff.

There is a reason for the fact that very little hospital food can be identified. If you don't know what you're eating, it is virtually impossible to complain about it. Therefore, the hospital kitchen receives few complaints and the De-appetizing Machines go into overdrive churning out hospital fare that would gag a maggot off a gut wagon.

You will find that most hospital food is designed around a product loosely described as jello. Actually, this dish of translucent latex is produced by the Goodyear Tire and Rubber Company under a contract dating back to the Civil War. Although it has virtually no nutritional value, and has all the sapidity attraction of rubber cement, jello has one quality that has long endeared it to the medical community: it is impossible to spill. Whereas just about anything else will slop over on its journey from scullery to sick bay, jello will not. Indeed, it can be dribbled down the hall and slam–dunked into a patient's lap without so much as missing a quiver. Its one redeeming quality is that it doesn't have to be mopped up.

If one does have the temerity to complain about the food, this automatically triggers a visit from the hospital dietician. This hapless person, generally female, can always be identified by an armadillo–like exterior, nature's way of warding off the slings and arrows of outraged patients. Dieticians work hand–in–glove with the cook who operates the De–appetizing Machine. Under the guise of producing food that is good for you, i.e., no fat, no salt, no cholesterol, no sugar, no seasoning, and above all, no flavor, these two conspirators get away with murder.

The maxim of the dietician is, "If it tastes good, spit it out."

Adding insult to injury, the nurse hovers over you while you both try to guess what you're eating. And she will insist that you clean your plate, no matter how green you get at the gills. If there is one incentive to get well in a hurry, eating hospital tray food is certainly it. The sooner you can become ambulatory, the sooner you can be weaned from the tray and can journey over to the hospital cafeteria. Since most of the hospital staff eat there, the food is not only a shade better but at times is even recognizable.

A caution is in order at this point: do not bow to your nurse's chidings of clearing your plate by stuffing the food into various cavities of your body while she isn't looking. Says Mabel Mammary of Leapfrog, Louisiana, "I had a most horrible experience when the doctor removed mah cast and saw that mah leg was kinda moldy and green–lookin'. He thought gangrene musta set in, and was jest about to

"Bon appetit, Mr. Throckmorton."

amputate when I finally confessed. I had stuffed what looked lak broccoli and turnip greens into mah cast, jest 'cause the nurse made me clean up mah plate. Lawzy me, I wasn't about to put any of that in mah mouth. That hospital food would make a gopher upchuck."

Adds LeRoy Lipshitz of New York, N.Y., "Get this. I survived hospital care because of my old buddy Quincy Cowlick. Quincy made a potted planter with a false bottom, just big enough to hold a hamburger. During visiting hours he would smuggle in a Big Mac disguised as a petunia plant. Thanks to McDonald's, I'm alive today. Later, Quincy patented his potted hamburger planter and is now worth millions."

"Reckon ah don't understand all this bad–mouthin' of hospital food," adds Pinto Pistolwhip of Swillwater, Texas. "Ah brought some home from the Saint Judas Hospital here in Swillwater, and left it lyin' around the kitchen. You know what? Killed every cockroach in the house. Been tryin' all mah life to get rid of those critters, some so big you could throw a saddle on. Ain't nothin' ever been able to kill a Texas cockroach before. But that hospital food sure done the trick. Yessiree, Bob!"

Unhappily, in medical circles just like anywhere else, it's the squeaky wheel that gets the grease. If you have been committed to the hospital for a lengthy stay, by squawking loudly enough you may be able to talk your physician into prescribing a pill designed to anesthetize your taste buds. Taking one before each meal may help you in getting your tray food down.

However, getting the food down is only half the battle. During its digestion phase, hospital victuals have been known to produce more gas than was contained in the Hindenburg zeppelin. And, to touch upon this subject as delicately as possible, this gas must be expelled, lest one assume the shape of the afore-mentioned airship.

Before one dismisses flatulence as being of little significance, a statement recently issued by John Trumble, of Boise, Idaho, is not to be ignored: "It has been recently reported that the flatulence of farm animals contributes 60 million tons of methane gas to the greenhouse effect annually, worldwide." The report goes on to suggest that farm animals should perhaps be equipped with 'cattlelytic' converters. And when you figure that humans outnumber cows a thousand to one, no wonder we have a greenhouse problem.

It has not been officially decreed as to just what extent hospital food contributes to the greenhouse effect, but there is no denying the other dangers inherent in the gaseous by–products of hospital fare. The author apologizes for dwelling on this indelicate problem; but it must not be ignored. This treatise will gladly bear the onus of questionable taste if it means protecting you from grievous harm.

In this regard it is prudent to heed the wisdom of one Clancy Bullbreath, veteran of eighteen hospital internments thanks to a rare social disease picked up on the island of Pago Pago. "My extensive hospital visits," says Bullbreath, "have etched into my brain two things: Never light up a cigarette when there's an oxygen tube stuck up your nose; or when there's a patient in the next bed suffering from extreme gastritis. I've learned the hard way the folly of pursuing either course of action."

Hospital explosions are not a pretty sight. When one occurs, the hospital spokesman always blames it on an oxygen leak, a natural gas leak, or spontaneous combustion. Never will it be admitted that in all likelihood the explosion was created by an unhappy union of hospital food effluvium and an open flame. Unfortunately, there is seldom a survivor who can attest to the contrary.

Thanks to *glasnost,* the truth can now come out about the so-called Russian nuclear disaster at Chernobyl. It was not a problem in the nuclear plant at all, but an explosion that took place in the nearby Chernobyl hospital. As everyone knows, there is nothing more volatile than the gas generated by eating cabbage soup. On the day of the explosion, Polish sausage and cabbage soup had been served for lunch at the Chernobyl Hospital. Unfortunately, shortly after lunch a new father came into the maternity ward and, to celebrate the arrival of his new son, lit a cigar. The rest is history. The borscht blowout leveled the hospital and did serious damage to the nearby nuclear plant.

Russian cooks are seldom mentioned among the Great Chefs of Europe anyway, and after this disaster, borscht has been considered along with mid–range missiles as a bargaining chip for world disarmament.

So, be on your toes (which is not difficult to do when suffering from acute gas accumulation) and be aware of this little–discussed malady.

"We used to have a daily contest," says Gladys Gasleak, 89, of Notus, Idaho. "The patient in our ward who could expel gas the longest continually while walking won the prize. I usually brought home the honor as I got so I could make one expulsion last all the way to the nurses' station and back. Not bad, considering the nurses' station was on the third floor and my ward was in the basement. But I'm afraid my success was short–lived. I was badly beaten out for the grand prize by Kaopectate Gonzales, a 400–pound Mexican, who continuously deflatulated clear to the roof fire escape and back. We later learned he won dishonestly, though, as his wife was smuggling him jalapeno peppers.

"Goodness gracious," added Gladys, fanning her forehead. "When I think of the fire hazard we generated, it almost makes me faint. Just one spark and the Good Samaritan and Eight–Lane Bowling Alley Hospital would have been blown to kingdom come."

In sum, we need not worry too much about the energy crisis. If push comes to shove, the gas created from the food served by even a small hospital, if properly harnessed, could light up a city the size of Detroit.

Again, the author apologizes for this seeming affront to rectitude and good taste. But if being properly forewarned of these pitfalls enhances in even a small way the pleasure of one's hospital stay, this scatological discussion will not have been presented in vain.

And ending this chapter on a bright note, some hospitals are now serving wine with their meals. This will do nothing to improve the taste of hospital food, but if the fermented grape is served in large enough quantities, the patient may not care quite so much that the food tastes like the bottom of a gerbil cage.

ROMANCING
YOUR BEDPAN

nce again, at the risk of flouting propriety, we must tackle a subject that is generally shied away from by Ms. Emily Post and her compatriots. However, elimination is a natural function, nearly all of us do it, and therefore must be handled in any worthwhile compendium of hospital activity. It will, of course, be treated with the same tact and dignity as the previous section in which we dealt so delicately with the issue of farting.

You will find that elimination, unhappily, will consume much of your attention during your hospital stay. Nurses and doctors can come up with the most embarrassing questions concerning your bowel habits, as if this scatological function has replaced sex as the main topic for conversation. And nothing will satisfy these nosey nabobs; your by–products are always too hard, too soft, too frequent, too seldom or too loose.

As Major Minor of Fort Ord, California, puts it, "You really can't say much for the mentality of hospital help when they take your bedpan and study it like a band of demented Gypsies trying to read tea leaves. After all, what do they expect to come out of that bilge they serve as hospital food—crushed pineapple?"

"I agree," says Ms. Lettice Goedebed of Hangtooth, Arizona. "These people are obsessed by potty–poo. It's almost like they were experimenting with some kind of new recycling program and couldn't wait to see the results."

Since so much time is devoted in hospitals to showcasing things we are accustomed to doing daily only in the privacy of our own bathroom, a rundown of hospital nomenclature might be helpful. This lexicon comes from Nurse Priscilla Pantzaroff of Goose Bay, Newfoundland. "There are many names for the same thing," says Nurse Pantzaroff, "depending upon what part of the country you hail from. The following list should help you understand what the nurse is saying, regardless of where you plant your roots.

"Number One is also known as Making Water, Going Tinkle, Hitting the Sandbox, Taking A Leak, Making Pee Pee, Doing Wet–Wet, Going Piddle, Relieving Oneself, or Making A Puddle.

"Number Two is known as Evacuation, Going Chair–Chair, Having a BM, Making Ka Ka, Taking an Arrofat, Doing the Big Job, Piling Doo Doo, or Having to Do Yucky Poo. So when the nurse mentions any of the above, you'll know what she' s talking about.

"Both numbers One and Two may be included in Using the Convenience, Visiting the Loo, Hitting the WC (Water Closet), Going Toidy, or Powdering One's Nose."

But a rose by any other name still smells, and in

this case it must be properly disposed of. This is most often accomplished by use of the bedpan, which, with the possible exception of the spiked Iron Maiden used by the inquisitioners in the Middle Ages, is the most fiendish instrument of torture ever designed by the hand of man.

Doctor Percival Philpott, in his highly–acclaimed doctoral dissertation, *Slopjars Through the Ages,* gives an exciting history of the honey bucket's evolution. For instance, very few people know that the commode was invented by one John Crapper, which is why people often refer to their bathroom fixture as "the John."

And it was the Honorable Dennis Dipstick, of England's conservative Tory Party, who did so much for the chamber pot by proclaiming, "Call it treason if you will, but I'd rather have a can of pee under me than a canopy over me."

Suffice it to say there have been dramatic changes in the bedpan since its inception in the Stone Age as a lopped–off coconut shell. Through its evolution as a porcelain thing of beauty, to today's state–of–the–art gleaming stainless–steel vessel complete with racy bright–red competition stripe, its egregious mission, however, has not changed over the years.

Although heavily romanticized in Bathsheba Klinkenberg's immortal "Ode to a Thundermug," the fact remains that the bedpan is simply not a bucket of yuks. At the risk of alienating the reader, this devil's plaything must be explored in depth as the first–time hospital patient must be made aware of its limitations and capabilities.

Today's patient will be happy to learn that modern hospitals seldom keep bedpans in the freezer anymore. Inserting a frozen bedpan under a patient's derriere has been used in the past not only as a form of torture, but as a disciplinary measure. This ghoulish instrument was first used by Hitler's Gestapo to extract information from recalcitrant war prisoners.

The frozen bedpan has also been used as punishment for incorrigible patients who insist on goosing their nurse, cracking walnuts with their cast, or trying to grope the volunteer candy–stripers. Now, happily, this form of torture has been outlawed by the Geneva Convention and has mostly gone the way of the Cat–o–nine–tails, blackboard scratching, and the release of white sharks in swimming pools.

Thanks to modern technology, there are new techniques that now compete with the bedpan. New hospital rooms have flushing commodes that pull down from the wall. Digital computers in the hospital bathrooms now weigh and analyze by–products. This boon dispenses with the messy measurements of the plastic urinal that decorates the roll bar of beds in backward hospitals, and the embarrassing questions regarding your body functions which are nobody's business but your own.

Yancey Yuck of Gargle, Louisiana, working on a Harvard grant, invented his Sizzling Slopjar. Wired up with 2,000 volts of electricity, this chamber pot instantly cremated its contents with no mess or odor, leaving only a small residue of ash. "Works great," announced Yuck at the Sizzling Slopjar's unveiling.

"Now all I have to do is figure out how to prevent third–degree burns in the areas of our body we do not mention in mixed company."

Doctor Desiree Deepthroat, also working on a college grant, spent thirty–two years developing a new kind of nutritious hospital food that resembled a graham cracker. Elimination was no problem, as all one needed was a whisk broom. Although promising, the success of this new product has been put on hold until the doctor can produce a graham cracker that doesn't taste like a graham cracker.

But regardless of how sophisticated we get in the art of waste disposal, consummating the evacuation act, along with eating hospital food, still remains high on the average hospital's agenda of problems. In spite of the new advances in the field, the function of the very latest technology is no better than the people operating it. It is, and will always be, subject to human error.

Case in point: "Thought I had it made in the shade," reports Earlybird Bellamy, of Isleton, California. "Was just recovering from a gall bladder transplant in one of San Francisco's finest hospitals and wasn't yet ambulatory. The nurse had helped me onto the latest state–of–the–art commode, then she immediately left the room. I had just finished satisfying nature's nudge when the system started to break down.

"My repeated pushing of the nurse's button elicited no response, of course. As I was in a private room, shouting was to no avail. After thirty minutes sitting on that torture rack, I found my legs were starting to turn blue and prompt remedial action was called for. Happily, I could reach the telephone. I dialed the hospital in which I was a patient and asked for the nurses' station on the fourth floor. When my nurse, Yetava Bilgebreath, finally answered, and I told her the patient in Room 412 would sure like to get off the bedpan, you can imagine her reaction."

"Never could understand," adds Seymour Sidebottom, a television executive in New York

City, "why nurses go to all the trouble of putting you on the pot, then promptly forget you. Fortunately, the TV in the nurses' center is tuned to my television station. I had to have one of my camera crews come to my room, take a live shot of me on the throne, and insert it into the five o'clock news before I got any attention from my nurse."

Various other techniques of getting the nurse's attention have been tried, with varying degrees of success. Federal Express, Fax machines and singing telegrams have all been used to vie for the nurse's attention. Perhaps the most effective method was used by Gadfry Gridlock of Winona, Wisconsin, who hired a skywriter to buzz the hospital and write out the words, "Gadfry's still on the pot."

As we pull the curtain down on this somewhat revolting yet necessary subject, it is hoped the reader will benefit from the experience of others, and will have a better understanding of the inner workings of our modern hospitals and their staffs. When it comes to bedpan elimination, Mr. Larry Lampoon of Gezundheit, Georgia, sums it up poetically in his treatise, *Getting the Most from Your Bedpan,* when he states, "You will never badmouth your bedpan if you just consider the alternative." A motto one would be well–advised to ponder.

As is the slogan emblazoned on the headquarters building of the National Nursing Foundation: "The Waste Is A Terrible Thing To Mind."

SHOULD YOU HAVE SEX
DURING SURGERY?

The question most asked by people contemplating a hospital stay of over 24 hours is, of course, "Is it all right to have sex in the hospital?"

The answer, naturally, is a resounding "Yes!"

Any self–respecting hospital is vitally concerned with the morale of its patients. What, therefore, could be a better contribution to a patient's well–being than an occasional frolic in the feathers?

Bud Shinnsplint, in his Pulitzer–prize–winning book, *Brothels and Bedpans,* sheds some very interesting historical light on sex and sickbays. It seems that the compatibility of the two have roots sunk deep in history. For instance, during the Civil War when Sherman was marching through Georgia, the first thing he looked for in every town he overran was the local house of ill–fame. The reason for this was two–fold, the second reason being the establishment of the house as a hospital for his wounded troops.

And what could be more logical? The house of shady ladies generally contained private cubicles, clean beds, water and washstands, lots of towels, and a staff of young ladies proficient in the arts of satisfying the needs of distressed men. The harlot house soon became the hospital—a natural evolution.

And it was General Joseph Hooker, another Civil War General, who allowed camp–followers to accompany his troops into battle where they could administer physical as well as social satisfaction, thereby bestowing the good general's name to ladies of negotiable virtue.

Thus, hospitals down through the ages have had a very close relationship with sex. It is not just happenstance that modern–day hospitals have private rooms, curtains that allow privacy in the wards, push–button beds that can assume wild and crazy configurations, hospital garb that can be dropped with one yank of a bow ribbon, acres of towels, and a nurse's call button that, when pushed, will guarantee solitude for hours. Truly, if there ever was a setting for unbridled hanky–panky, today's hospital is it.

And to really put the frosting on the cake, it is no accident that visiting hours have been established to include a large part of the evening. This gives one a chance to cohabit with one's spouse, mistress or lover. Or all three. But if you can't be near the one you love, you may love the one you're near by sharing your rubber sheets with an off–duty nurse, the ward custodian, the night nurse, the dietician, the day nurse, the book–cart lady, the head nurse, or the vending–machine stocker.

If none of these blossom your bloomers, there are always the visitors–hordes of love–starved people who gather like lovelorn lemmings during visiting hours, eager to fluff the goose down with hospital patients. "Sure beats the single's bars for meeting people," says Lorelei Lovelace of Tin Pan, Tennessee. "I went into the hospital for a liposuction of my bottom and checked out with two proposals of marriage, a new husband, and a steady boyfriend. Turns out these visitors knew no one in the hospital, they just went there to meet people."

"I used to go to the bowling alley to meet women," said bashful Eureka Foamblower of Saddlepouch, Saskatchewan. "But hospitals beat 'em all hollow. Beauty is, you just tell people you came to visit your fiancee down the hall and you'd just learned she'd passed away. Where else can you sit on the edge of a pretty girl's bed while she clasps you to her bosom in sympathy and feeds you orange juice? Our lady of the Swamp Hospital here in Saskatchewan even has single's night visiting hours every Thursday. It was there I met my third wife, who was recovering from a weird accident caused by sitting down unexpectedly. She was a professional sword–swallower."

Armed with the knowledge that sex is not only allowed, but definitely encouraged in modern hospitals, here are a few suggestions that will help you along the pathway of erotic fulfillment:

1. Sex is seldom encouraged during surgery, especially if it's with the surgeon. It has a tendency to take the doctor's mind off his work.

2. Sex should also be discouraged immediately after surgery as this could conceivably rip your stitches. If your passion cannot be contained during this period, you might consider having your surgeon seal you up with Velcro.

3. Care should be exercised with the push–button beds. During carnal congress, a patient got her toe caught in the push–button and before anyone could stop it, the bed closed up like a clamshell. The hapless patient had to be surgically removed from an encyclopedia salesman.

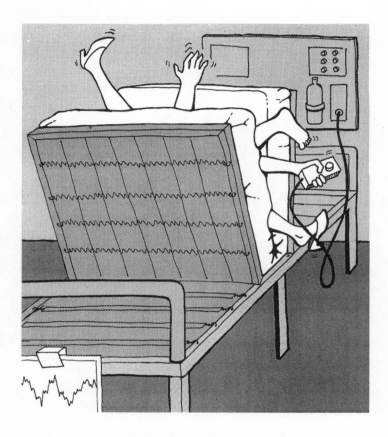

*Know your hospital–bed buttons before
trying hanky panky with your nurse.*

4. If one is wearing a cast, caution should be exercised during foreplay. Caught up in the rapture of the moment, a visitor was nearly cold–cocked by a wild–swinging arm cast.

5. If you and your inamorata are both wearing casts, be sure your plaster of Paris has thoroughly dried. A recent report discloses that two patients in adjoining beds were a bit premature in their expressions of undying love; their wet plaster fused, and they had to be separated a week later with dynamite.

6. Patients over 80 should make sure the guard rail on the bed is in the UP position and locked. Lyceum Lovetonsils of Fireplug, Florida, put it this way. "I knew we shoulda had the guard rail up, but that Jeremiah was the sexiest ninety–year–old I ever did see. I just wish that when we fell outta the bed he hadn't landed on top of me 'cause I checked in with a hammertoe and checked out with a pancaked pancreas." She sighed ecstatically. "But it was sure worth it."

It is hoped that this brief chapter will assuage any of your fears of a celibate stay in the hospital. Just be sure you pack your deodorant, your cologne and/or shaving lotion.

It's a good idea to stay well–groomed, for it's quite possible you might find yourself sharing your eggshell mattress with someone you know.

"Well Doctor Proctor made the *New England Journal of Medicine* and I ended up with a nice thatch of hair. I have to admit it's an improvement, once you get used to green hair. Only problem is, people keep trying to stick a golf tee in my scalp."

Still another reason for questionable operations is due to the vanity of patients. Ms. Mywot Boobs of Cloverdale, Connecticut, illustrates. "I have no one but myself to blame for my unusual situation," says Ms. Boobs. "But I was a TV anchorwoman and I had to look sharp to keep my job. As you know, anchorwomen may have a low IQ as long as they have a high bra size.

"Anyway, I had so many facelifts, my mouth ended up on the top of my head. Being a heavy smoker, this presented a problem as people kept throwing their drinks on me, thinking my hair was on fire." She shook her head sadly. "It did have one salutary side effect. I could put my lunch in my hat and eat it on the way to work."

Says Bombastic Breakwind of La Junta, Colorado,

"I'll have to admit I had to go to Tijuana, Mexico, to find a doctor who would do my operation, but it had to be done. You see, I was a salesman for a pharmaceutical firm that manufactured decongestant cold tablets. Well, I have an awful sinus problem that is continually draining through this big, red, runny nose of mine. As you can imagine, it was tough to convince customers that our decongestant cold tablets were the best on the market when I was dripping like Niagara Falls. So I had this bright idea.

"Doctor Conchita Cucaracha transplanted my nose to my armpit and put a handsome plastic nose in its place. Now, my real nose is out of sight; it can drip all it wants and I can blow it by just flapping my arm. It's a Godsend, and my business is booming. Only drawback, I have to use a strong underarm deodorant, or on a hot day—well, we won't go into that."

Says Dinsmore Dogdoo of San Bernardino, California, "My doctor was an amateur inventor and thanks to him, I now lead a very productive life. I lost both legs in an uneven contest with a wheat com-bine. Since I was a mailman, this kind of put a crimp in my livelihood. Then I went to see Doc Frankensteen. Doc fashioned me a pair of light–metal legs, wired with a battery that could put out about 50 volts.

"Well, as you know, the mortal enemy of the mailman is the neighborhood dog. If I had a buck for every time I got bit, I'd be a millionaire. Any-way, I now run my own Rent–A–Mailman business. In cities that have a real neighborhood–dog prob-lem, I hire out to take the mail route. When a dog attacks, I just electrify my leg and the hound really gets a charge out of that. Hard to bite someone when your teeth are fused. Believe me, after that shocking experience a dog won't attack another mailman."

He chuckled. "Never will forget the time a French poodle lifted his leg on my trousers with the current on. When last seen, the mutt was passing through Fairbanks, Alaska, doing about ninety miles an hour. You betcha. Doc Frankensteen really gave me a new lease on life."

Another daring first that made the medical journals was when Doctor Sikh Andhye of Harvard Medical School successfully completed the first X–ray corneal implant. The patient was Sorghum Gumdrop of Bilgebucket, South Carolina. "I'm an X–ray technician," states Sorghum, "and when my eyes went bad, I thought I'd get X–ray implants, which would be a big help in my work. They work fine, except I can see right through cloth and everybody looks naked as a barber pole. At first it was kind of fun, but believe me, more people look better with clothes on than with clothes off. Didja ever go around mentally *dressing* people?"

Says Cyrano Grabcrotch of Why, Arizona, "The old ticker decided to go on a rampage. I've always had arrhythmia, which is why I'm such a good dancer, but last month the arrhythmia got carried away, went into fibrillation and, as we all know, after about four minutes of this, we're talking wormchow.

"Three times we ended up calling the paramedics and, although their teams are fantastic, they always bring the firemen with them. And firemen like to keep their hand in by opening front doors with fireaxes. So after replacing three front doors, I decided it was time to do something. I held a meeting with my cardiac consultants and they came up with three options:

"One, do nothing and carry the phone around, finger poised to dial 911. (This option was abandoned when the paramedics threatened to get an unlisted number.) Two, try to tame the arrhythmia with drugs. Problem here is that the drugs are so toxic, they have been known to make nuns pregnant and people pass gas in church. Third option, implant an AICD.

"Now the AICD (Automatic Implantable Cardioverter Defibrillator) is the greatest space–age invention since the portable bidet, is implanted in the abdomen, and is a little larger than a deck of cards. With leads fastened to the heart, it monitors the heart's pulse rate and when the ticker needs a

85

kicker, it zaps the heart until it resumes its normal rhythm. This little medical toy costs about 50 grand installed, batteries not included.

"Everyone should have one. I take off my shirt on our patio and it makes one helluva bug–zapper. The new model will be equipped with a jump–cable for starting cars with dead batteries.

"And there's the true story about the man who had an AICD implanted and found himself in a particularly romantic mood. He talked his spouse into a bit of hanky–panky and things were going swimmingly when just at the height of his passion, his AICD fired. Embarrassed as hell, he was trying to uncurl his toes while fanning away the smoke puffing out of his wife's navel. Stifling her husband's apologies, she said, 'Sorry, hell! How do we adjust that sucker so it'll do it every time?' "

These are just a few interesting offbeat operations that have taken place. With the continued march of medical technology, there will be many that are even more far–out. On the drawing board now are two state–of–the–art robots designed for space travel. Called ADAM, M–1 (Astronomically Designed Aerospace Man, Model No. 1) and EVE, M–2 (Electronic Virginal Environment, Model No. 2), these two androids are designed to live in space, and come complete with such options as nylon hair, naugahyde wrinkle–proof skin, push belly–button cigarette lighter, and arthritic–free hydraulics. All they now lack are the human brains needed to activate them.

So be forewarned when you discuss operation options with your doctor. He could be feathering his nest or trying to make the medical journals. Or there's even a remote chance that he might be trying to improve your medical well–being. Anything is possible. But be especially cautious if a medic approaches you with a proposition for a brain transplant. You just might end up in an operation that's really far–out.

Says Ms. Poplin Joplin of Jerome, Pennsylvania, "I've been leery of doctors ever since I had that problem with a buzzing in my abdomen, and an unaccountable compulsion to go to the phone. After six months of therapy with my shrink, I discovered that ole Doc Neffertiti had sewed up his beeper in my stomach during a gallstone operation. Can you imagine? My gallstones still act up every time the phone rings."

And not to be taken lightly is the report from Hyacinth Hotbreath of Meringue, Montana, who relates her sad case with Dr. Sylvester Sheepdip. "I checked into the hospital with a broken toe, flopping around like an old layer hen with a broken egg bag. They got it fixed up, and then I came down with a bad case of Dutch Elm's disease from the doc's tongue depressor. Hospitals just ain't safe."

So above all, keep a cool head and don't panic over these little adversities. For what else can you expect from a profession that conducts operations on men and calls them *her*nias, and conducts operations on women and calls them *his*torectomies?

THE DAY
OF
RECKONING

Finally, we come to the Day of Reckoning: the day you check out of the hospital and are presented with The Bill. And believe me, there will be no checking out until The Bill is satisfied.

Indeed, Melba Mayhatch, a case–worker from Moosetooth, Minnesota, reports on one of her charges who checked into the hospital with a 24–hour flu bug and ended up staying three years before she saved enough money from her social security checks to bail herself out of the hospital.

"It was awful," reports Ms. Mayhatch, "they had that poor lady shoveling guano down in the basement. When they finally released her, she had to check right back into the hospital for an eye operation. After three years down in the basement cave, she emerged as blind as a bat. It was terrible!"

Another point that most people find hard to believe: some hospitals don't make money. In spite of handing out bills that would underwrite Zsa Zsa Gabor's fanny tucks, many of our medical sanctuaries are operating in the red.

This explains why you'll now find hospitals with strange–sounding names, the result of merging with other businesses in an attempt to reduce the overhead. Madam Graballi's Mustang Ranch and Mercy Hospital, and Reno's Sweet Bliss Wedding Chapel and Infirmary are two examples of unions blessed by the IRS. To be avoided, however, are hospitals bearing such sobriquets as the Sisters of Mercy Hospital and Crematorium, or the Heavenly Angels Hospitals and Cat Food Company—both of which can get you coming or going.

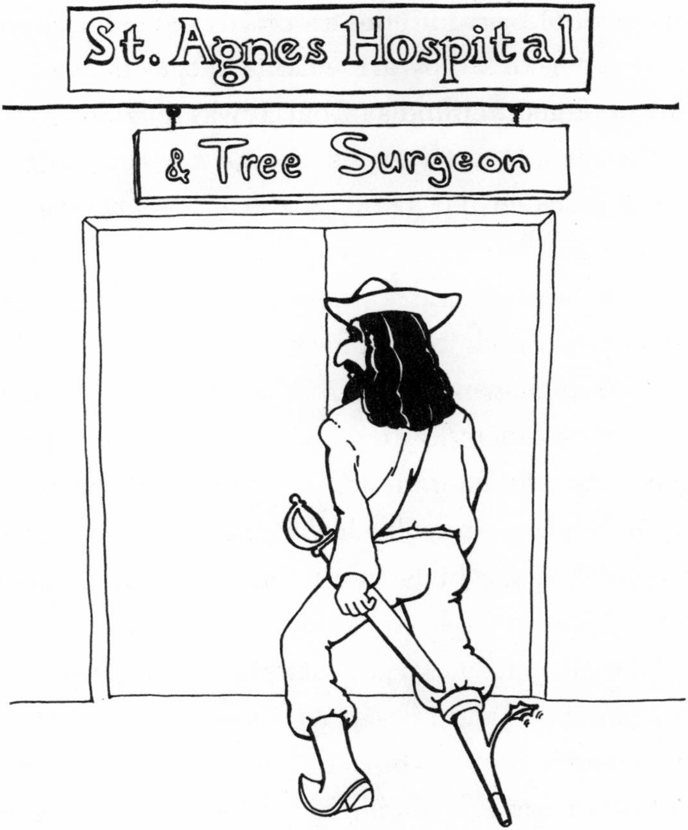
St. Agnes Hospital
& Tree Surgeon

And since some hospitals (unlike most brothels) have trouble making ends meet (you should pardon the expression), they are making extraordinary efforts to keep their beds filled, especially with well–heeled people like yourself. Farrah Fawcett Fudge, in her shocking expose *Confessions of a Nympho Nurse,* relates the following:

"I know of two cases where patients were kept in the hospital just because they had lots of money. The Holy Hemlock and Open Air Fish Market Hospital was not exactly rolling in dough, you might say. The first patient to fall into their clutches was Fanny Fedora, a widow whose husband made tons of money by replacing the high–caloric olive in your martini with a glass marble.

"Unfortunately, Mr. Fedora choked to death on one of his marbles but left his Fanny very wealthy. She checked into the hospital with a strange allergy and they managed to keep her in a private room for 28 years.

"She fixed her room up real nice; there not being too many hospital rooms that contain a Jacuzzi, bidet, wet bar and pool table. They never did find the cause of her allergy, though, until her autopsy. Seems she was allergic to the rubber foam in hospital pillows. They put a nice plaque on the door of her room and put her ashes in a decorative vase right next to the fire extinguisher."

Says Sassafras Spasm from Hush Puppy, South Carolina, "The real reason you are always released from the hospital in a wheel chair is because most patients are still reeling from the computerized two–by–four administered by the accounting department. My husband, Cuthbert, was admitted to the Mount Holy Baptist Skating Rink and General Hospital here in Hush Puppy suffering from a most unfortunate accident. He's a demolition man and when he blew up the old ice–house here in town, the building fell on him. When they found him a week later, every bone in his body was broken. But thanks to the

Mount Holy Baptist Skating Rink and General Hospital, danged if they didn't get him all patched up again.

"He was in the hospital six months. Then, ya know what? The day he was released he took one look at his hospital bill, had a heart attack, and died right there on the spot. Ain't that the limit?"

Therefore, it is not recommended that you try to audit your bill yourself. In the first place, you shouldn't be lifting objects weighing over thirty pounds right out of the hospital, and secondly, only an accountant can figure out why one aspirin cost two dollars, a single Kleenex cost fifty cents, and each toilet flush is billed at one dollar.

Instead, just sign over a lien on your house, your car, your children, your Dinah Shore record collection, and let them take what they need. It is much less painful in the end.

BACKWORD

In closing, this guide would be incomplete if it did not include a couple of final items germane to the enjoyment of a rollicking romp in the hospital.

First, it is important that you learn a few medical terms with which to impress your hospital staff. It's not necessary to know the meanings of these terms, but rattling off a bit of medical jargon from time to time will separate you from the first–timers, the neophytes who are fair game for the white–frockers. By checking in with an aura of experience, you will find that you are not quite such an easy target for indifference and inefficiency.

Herewith are a dozen medical terms that should be memorized and will show your hospital attendants that you are no stranger to the medical world. Although some doctors may claim that these words have their roots in some kind of Latin geneology, the nurses will staunchly claim that the following translations of these terms are correct.

- Infarction: A by–product of eating too many frijoles.
- Mammygram: A telegram to Eddie Cantor's mom.
- Cardiology: The art of poker playing.
- Endocarditis: The poker game's been raided.
- Polyunsaturated: When Polly was a virgin.
- Angina Pectoris: A nasty phrase dealing with sex whatnots.
- Cat Scan: Checking your cat for fleas.
- Pulmonary Artery: An Amtrak route that has a sleeper car.
- Ventricles: Part of a man's public region that makes seamen.
- Euthanasia: An idyllic world where all youth is sent to Asia.

- Eustachian Tube: Something you tie when you don't want any more babies.
- Walletectomy: You'll know when you pay your hospital bill.
- Hippocratic Oath: A swear word the surgeon uses when he finds he's sewed his thumb to your epiglottis.

As stated, by occasionally salting your conversation with a bit of medical rap, you will be immediately recognized as a hospital veteran, and one who is not to be trifled with.

If you are contemplating elective surgery, the financial instability of some hospitals can be a blessing. Like considering any other major expenditure, it is wise to shop around. Bargains are out there, so it behooves you to do your homework.

"I live in a town of very competitive hospitals," says Gloria Gallstone of Houston, Texas. "I needed a hemorrhoidectomy, so I put my butt out to bid, if you'll pardon the indelicacy. Bids from three different hospitals were miles apart. I finally went with the Houston Oil Rigging and Obstetrics Medical Center. They not only came in with the lowest bid, but they threw in a nose job, a tonsillectomy, and an oil change. I was really sore on both ends for a while, but it shows how it pays to shop around."

"You should watch the paper for specials," agrees Doris Droopybosom of Sarasota, Florida. "On Thursday nights they have an Early–Bird Special on bunionectomys. Wednesday night is Senior Citizen Night, and you can have your knee caps pulled up out of your socks on a two–for–one sale. Sunday is nice, if you have a wattleectomy they throw in a candle–light pizza dinner for two.

"You might say Sarasota's kind of an old–poops' hangout just because we have three–wheeled bicycle races and carry a prune–juice flask to the Saturday night dances. But our social life is second to none and I'll bet our funerals are the liveliest in the whole state of Florida. About the only thing that flopped here was the Sarasota Three–Ring Circus and Funeral Parlor. They advertised two–for–one casket sales and an enticing lay–away plan. But for some reason it never caught on like our hospital bargains."

Even doctors' fees are negotiable. Just be leery of a doctor who wants to be paid up front. This just might indicate that the good medic may have doubts as to his ability to pull you through. Anesthesiologists are notorious for trying to sock it to you. If they try to slip you your bill while you're still unconscious, have none of it. And never hire a medical practitioner who will not include a warranty good for at least six months or six thousand miles.

So, there you have it. Armed with all of this knowledge gleaned from hospital patients from the four corners of the globe, you will be well prepared for your hospital stay.

Body pricking, blood–letting, bedpan–using, bone–setting and open–heart surgery can be enjoyed to the max if approached with the right attitude. And now that you know what goes on behind closed doors, what is expected of you and your hospital staff, you have become a well–greased cog that will mesh nicely into the system.

Not only will you survive hospital care, you will come through with flying colors like the champion you are. So look at the bright side, and always remember: that urine specimen jar is not half–empty, it is half–full.

With that upbeat attitude, hospital stays can be more fun than a barrel of monkeys. And on top of all that . . .

You get breakfast in bed.

ABOUT THE AUTHOR

William C. Anderson has not only frolicked through open–heart surgery on several occasions, but has made the medical journals by being the first person to have his tonsils removed rectally with a pair of Basque sheep–shearing shears.

It was only natural, therefore, that this distinguished author and screen–writer address his talents to the production of this sorely–needed primer on how to survive hospital care.

Mister Anderson lives in Boise, Idaho with his lovely wife, Dortha. They have three grown children, all of whom are allergic to penicillin.

ALSO BY
WILLIAM C. ANDERSON

Penelope
ADAM, M-I
Pandemonium On the Potomac
The Gooney Bird
The Two-Ton Albatross
The Apoplectic Palm Tree
Roll Up the Wall Paper, We're Moving
Hurricane Hunters
The Headstrong Houseboat
The Great Bicycle Expedition
Penelope, The Damp Detective

When the Offspring Have Sprung:
Happiness Is Turning the Nursery Into a Wine Cellar

Home Sweet Home Has Wheels:
Please Don't Tailgate the Real Estate

BAT-21
Bomber Crew 369
Taming Mighty Alaska
Lady Bluebeard

Did You Borrow This Book?
Want A Copy of Your Own?

Makes a Great Gift for a Friend or Loved One.

To order *How To Survive Hospital Care*
call 1-800-358-1929

Have your VISA or MasterCard ready, or use this order form.

Name _____
   please print

Address _____

City _____ **State** _____ **Zip** _____

Total Copies x $6.95 each:		
Sales Tax, @ $0.35/copy: *(Idaho Residents Only)*		
Shipping and Handling ($2.00 each)		
Grand Total		

Please make check or money order payable to Legendary Publishing for amount in Grand Total box, and send to the address below. Or use your VISA or MC by writing your card number and signing below.

Credit Card #: _____

❏ **VISA**   ❏ **MC**

Signature _____ **Exp. Date** _____

MAIL TO:
Legendary Publishing Company
P.O. Box 7706 Boise, Idaho 83707-1706
For bulk discount prices, call 1-800-358-1929. Quantity orders invited.